Professional Love

Professional Love

ProLove

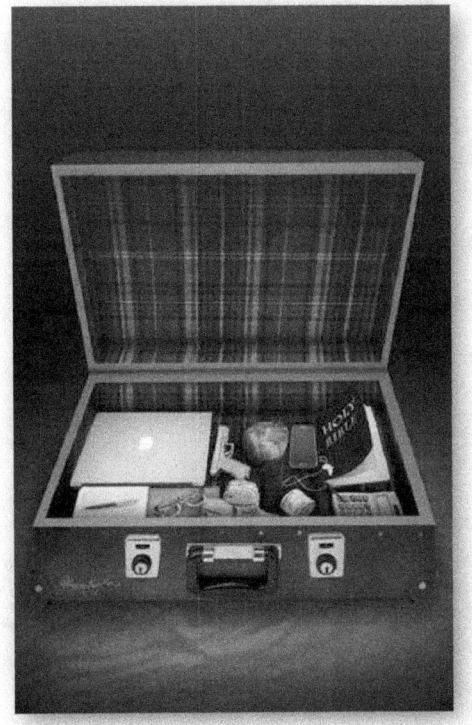

Adrian "Ace" Martin

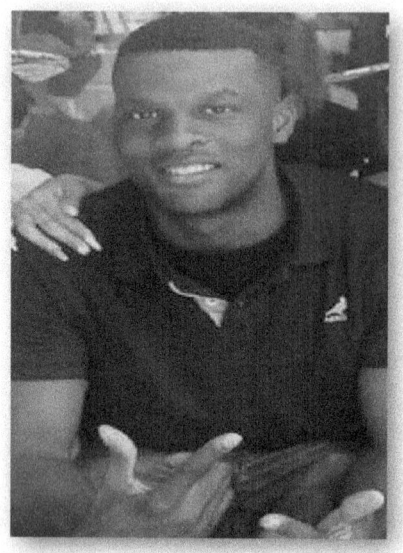

Copyright © 2016 by Adrian "Ace" Martin
ISBN: 1533023425
ISBN 13: 9781533023421
Library of Congress Control Number: 2016912158
CreateSpace Independent Publishing Platform
North Charleston, South Carolina

Ordering Information:
Quantity sales. Special discounts are available on quantity purchases by corporations, associations, and others. For details or purchases, contact the publisher at ace_martin_t@yahoo.com. Orders by US trade bookstores and wholesalers available and open. Printed in the United States of America

In Loving Memory Of
Christopher Terrell

Adrian has a degree in arts and a degree in business. He has produced several creative projects, from music and photography to short films. You name it; he probably has his hands in or around that atmosphere of art. He has been labeled a creative genius. He has traveled all over the world and is very culturally informed. He's a proud member of Phi Beta Sigma Fraternity Inc. and has also served his country proudly for ten years in the military with a deployment under his belt. It's easy to say he is a future leader in society. Please enjoy the moments of pleasure and pain with Adrian Martin.

All these poems are based on real life events.

Thank you for purchasing *Professional Love*. Please enjoy!

This Is For

Ace Boogie, all the soldiers lost in the struggle, poetry lovers, those who need guidance, people who believe in me, a good friend by the name of Raquel Rogers, and all the people who have been doubted in pursuit of their goals or dreams. I feel sometimes like I'm the only one of my peers left standing in this field of dreams and ambitions, so I tried my best to represent for those who can't be here with us. The love I have for writing is indescribable, although I was first known as an artist/producer. It's a struggle in itself to survive the nights and incidents that I had in my life, and I shall not be taken lightly in this form of artistry. Immediately after graduating from college, I worked several jobs at the same time. Some were great and some were terrible, but through it all, I found myself becoming frustrated because I wasn't able to vent my artistic flow, so I began to write my thoughts into poems. It instantly became a hobby, and my new level of maturity increased over the years. I remember sitting at my desk at work saying, "Wow! How cool would it be if we all could become professionals at the things we love to do?" I thought how cool it would be to escape the social norm of just working to being more passionate about the things that we actually love doing. We all reach a point in life where we battle professionalism versus love. On these lyrics I have cried tears, thrown things out of anger, had laughter, made love, and spilled soda. People will tell you not to follow your heart, but to follow a steady paycheck. Ladies and Gentlemen, for that, I introduce to you *Professional Love*. All glory goes to God.

Contents

This Is For · ix

Professional Love ·1
I Still Ain't Forgave Myself ·3
Space and Time ·5
Waiting on You—The Waiter ·7
Miss Africa—Dear Africa ·9
Dive—The Diver · 11
Makeup Does You No Good · 13
Love's Interlude · 14
The CEO—The Meeting · 15
The CEO Part II—After the Meeting · · · · · · · · · · · · · 16
And You Wonder Why · 18
Free Wi-Fi · 19
Dopeboy · 20
My Resume · 22
What Don't You See · 23
Black Bird · 24
Can I be your Mechanic?—The Mechanic · · · · · · · · · · · 25

In the House· ·26
I Ain't Your Toy ·28
Black Power ·29
Hot Pursuit—The Getaway ·31
F' Me ·33
Hell Nawl ·35
I Don't Know If I'm Ready ·36
Cocaine—Confessions of a Sex Junkie · · · · · · · · · · · · · ·38
I Never Would've Thought ·40
For One Night ·42
If All Women Were Like Oprah ·44
Diamond ·46
How Can I Not Shine ·48
Mr. Glass· ·50
Malcolm X—The Role Model· ·52
Don't Cry When It Gets Hard ·54
She Wasn't Ready ·56
Red, White, & Blue· ·58
I Will Always Love You ·60
No Longer ·62
The Janitor ·63
Send Me ·64

Professional Love

Find something you're willing to live for
then die for it.
I said, find something you're willing to live for then die for it.
Professionalism is often thought of as having a suit or dress on with clean
teeth followed by a great fragrance.
But that's just the upside of things.
You see, what about those who went nights without food to put in they
belly?
What about those who suffered financially to graduate college?
What about those who had to catch rides to and from work for a long period
of time?
Sometimes they whole day was a struggle, but they boss wouldn't let 'em
speak their mind—but they remained
professional. If you approach life
with great drive and ambition to succeed in certain things in life, then in
my eyes, you a professional. You don't realize how hard you had to work,
nor do you realize how much you had to believe in yourself to make these
things happen.
You don't have expensive clothes
with nice jewelry to match it,
but your faith, dreams, ideas, and passions will push you further in life
than most.
Professionalism isn't just in physical appearance or how you carry yourself;
it's also a state of mind.
Every day for at least twelve years, 365 days within those years,

parents have to grind for kids;
then folks want to talk crazy
and tell you how it is.
Sometimes to keep from choking somebody you have to bite your tongue,
and sometimes you have to be a professional to keep from crying,
because without professionalism, a lot of our enemies would be dying.
Remain professional and keep a heart of a lion.

I Still Ain't Forgave Myself

My brother's wife had a miscarriage when they came to my birthday party.
Although it happened before the party,
I still ain't forgave myself.
My other brothers got locked up while I was overseas chasing that government cheese...maybe if I was there, they would've had what they need.
For that I still ain't forgave myself.
She was a good girl
who I spoiled chasing that bad life,
and for that, man, I still ain't forgave myself.
When I was in these streets doin' music, I was making moves and gaining unwanted attention.
Two clubs got shot up; people even died...and for that I still ain't forgave myself.
As youth we was busting .38 specials on the playground
'cause we thought it was cool and liked the way it sound.
We lost a lot of homies to the struggles of these streets,
so I stay strapped like baby seats so
I won't be caught slipping in this heat.
I still ain't forgave myself.
I had sex with a married woman,
and for that I still ain't forgave myself.
I was trying to slang ye it wasn't a lot, but it would damn sure get you more than time in a day.
Every action has a repercussion,
and the consequences of my actions

have assisted in broken homes, drug addictions, and malnutrition.
I done a lot; I just hope you don't judge,
but that you would listen.
I done some things where I should be in the penitentiary.
I survived tragic events where others were put out they misery,
but God got me here as a blessing,
and I ain't proud of my mistakes,
but my HEART STRONG cause it had to carry so much weight.
I mourn for love 'cause I have experienced so much hate,
but since Jesus came to help,
ain't a damn reason why I still shouldn't FORGIVE MYSELF
...but I still haven't.

Space and Time

Babe, sit, so I can dig deeper than
between your inner thighs.
Your body is amazing,
and I'm mesmerized.
Only thing here is
space and time.
Society is all blind.
I'm on my knees praying to God
that I can keep his sweet angel with a perfect design.
But she say I'm not her type, so she can't be mine.
If she'd only give me a chance,
everything would've been fine.
We could be divine.
But she's making love to the money,
so I must be out of
my goddamn mind!
To think a girl like
this can be stimulated in mind
when so many guys grasp
the contour lines of her spine.
She's lost, and I'm
running outta time.
She's going the wrong direction,
and love is blind.
She follows the sounds

that sound unkind
but screams in agony
when she can't turn around,
married to a clown
who beats her down
when all she had to do
was walk on faith and turn around.
If you love someone,
don't let them go down.

Waiting on You—The Waiter

Is it dine in or carry out?
Please hurry! Because I don't have the time to be waiting on you.
You see, if you carry out,
you will only get a partial experience of what I have to offer...
However, if you choose to stay, you will feel an extreme aura of love and
respect that I will dedicate to you and only you.
Because I don't have anybody else;
I'm committed to giving you all this service...
Although it's easy to get
involved with everybody else,
I take pride in my myself and my work, so Imma focus all my time on you.
But if you leave, I'll let you go.
But you'll be begging to come back
because nobody else can do what I do or even think about doing it how I
do it.
You can go all over town
dragging your name in the dirt,
but they won't show you love or respect.
Please dine in, 'cause I'd love to spark your interest in casual conversation
about life and goals.
We don't have to talk about sex;
I wouldn't dare make you uncomfortable like that.
You see, my goal is to make you feel special, like the person you are.
I will accept you for who you are.
I won't push you to be somebody you ain't.

But look, I like you and all,
but I ain't got time to be waiting.
So what's it gonna be,
dine in or carry out?
'Cause unfortunately, life is too short;
I don't got time to be waiting on you.

Miss Africa—Dear Africa

As a BLACK man
in society, I cried many nights.
Of these nights I cried,
I pictured what Africa has gone through.
All the men who would have shaped her future were taken away.
She is the mother of ALL, including North America, who hates her...
North American babies have taken money up for years promising relief to
Africa from her critical condition,
but we all know Africa never gets the relief...even though she's in pain.
Sadly, in Africa, her children fight one another over money and land...
Africa once made kings and queens
who were murdered and raped cold blooded.
Do any of you shed tears for Africa like I do? 'Cause Lord knows I shed tears
for Africa!
Africa is the mother of all, but she is constantly robbed of jewelry and oil
as black as her skin.
It's a shame the same mother that loves us is abused.
Lord knows I shed tears for Africa.
Could you even imagine having your kids taken far away, never to return?
And when they do decide to return, they are hated by brothers and sisters
who think they abandoned the family...
but the truth is, they were captured into slavery for a great amount of time,
forced to have sex, beaten, manipulated, miseducated,
unappreciated, disoriented, devastated, some castrated, told they'd never
make it, not realizing who their real mother is and that greatness is within,

*so they live a life full of self-hating and sin thinking drugs, sex, and vio-
lence is where we began...it's up to me and you to tell these Negus they
can win!*

*I'm related to those brothers and sisters who were taken; to say I ain't mad
would be faking.*

I shed tears for Africa!

Just look at what you did to my mother.

*Since she ain't around, I got a mean sister and brother 'cause look what you
did to our mother!*

*Truthfully, I know where to find her, but look how much time has changed;
things wouldn't be the same.*

Many walk around hysterical, America,

misguided and institutionalized to suppress royalty...

but how could we be mad?

Look at what you did to our mother...

Dive—The Diver

Michael Phelps ain't got
nothing on me.
I said Michael Phelps ain't
got nothing on me!
I'm so talented,
and I will swim across
any lake, ocean, pond, or pool with excellence.
But playing in an ocean ain't particularly
what I like to do.
I think about all the sharks, whales, and things that've been in there, and
ha…that just ain't safe.
When everything and everybody has been in there, I have my doubts wheth-
er it's safe or not,
but if I see that it hasn't been exhausted, I might dive in.
But my ideal swim is in a nice clean pool that's under good care…
If you're willing, we can go for a swim. I'll show you just how I dive,
driving you into a euphoria.
I can start by playing on the surface,
just to arouse your thoughts.
I'm sure you would like that.
However you like it is the way I'll do it.
So, how do you like it?
I can dive in headfirst and get you all wet and excited.
I can get in that pool and swim shallow;
when the time is right, I'll go deeper

until you scream for me to come back or until you emotionally explode.
Truthfully, when I go swimming, I like others to feel my shockwaves through
the water...
I love to see the waves rock back and forth...it's so simple, but I love it,
and I'd like to caution you: if you go swimming with the wrong person,
you could get hurt.
Damn! Just let me be the one to take you there...let me be your life-
guard—you may think you're gonna drown,
but that's part of going down.
I'll surely lead you to safety...
I don't want anything but your time,
and if you give it, I'll teach you more than how to swim...
It really does excite me,
but I'll take my time, 'cause I ain't in a rush to dive in.

Makeup Does You No Good

I've been with women like you before:
You're in the mirror all day and night.
You're so selfish...
The men who would treat you right, you run them over.
I recall being in a relationship so bad
with you, I thought about getting high.
A couple of my friends would say it ain't a bad idea, but I don't smoke.
Anywayyyyyy, the focus is the woman in the mirror who is so self-centered
she hurts the men who would give her the world just to see her in her fuckin'
makeup. After us men fall into the trap.
We realize that makeup is only a mask...a DECOY.
Sadly we are often caught by the flesh:
the bodily features that deviate us from what's really on the inside.
God knows I was hurt...
Some nights I even cried.
It's like good men chase bad women, and good women chase bad men.
There are terrible people out there.
I thought it was easier, but the better I became, the worse it got...there are
women who sit in the mirror and practice fake smiles
to gain access to your assets.
Or land a spot on Love & Hip Hop.
My negus, be careful: that makeup won't do you no good.
I just don't want what happened to me to happen to you...but I'm sure
you'll learn.

Love's Interlude

How could I be so stupid...this chick's name was Love.

No bullshit—her real name was Love; while we were in college, we got aquainted.

She was there when I cried; she was there when I just needed somebody. I called her when I needed help, wanted to laugh, just to hear her voice, and, lastly, when I decided to leave my crazy, cheating girlfriend.

'Cause I knew she was a great person who would listen and help me cope.

Love was really there for me...secretly I wanted Love...and she knew it.

I was just waiting for the right time to speak my mind...

Sadly, I never left my crazy, cheating girlfriend...because I thought she was Love...which was a big mistake.

I told Love, and she took me for a joke.

Since then, we never spoke. I'm not sure why I completely lost her—maybe it's 'cause I was so stupid, maybe 'cause she was hurt, or 'cause I inbox her an Interlude song

that made me think of her while I was kinda still in a relationship.

But to this day, still no answer, and I may never know why.

But, ironically, the closest thing to love was a chick named Love, whom I never got the chance to love...

The CEO—The Meeting

Good morning, and greetings.
I'm glad you all could make this meeting.
But I'm frustrated that some of you are here.
Unfortunately, I know that's business.
However, this is unfair.
As a BLACK man, I built this empire
from hard work and dedication.
Then I look across the table and see some of you have cheated, hoe hopped,
and brownnosed your way to the top, and it ain't fair.
I have nothing against you;
I just feel that we are not equivalent.
If you're from the streets, you would say I got it out the mud
if you collect something from the mud.
Could you imagine the risk...
Truthfully you will get dirty,
but there is risk you might fall.
If you cheated your friends and family,
how can I be so sure you won't cheat me?
I'm the CEO, and you're fired!

The CEO Part II—
After the Meeting

Good afternoon, babe.
I just fired half my staff
because they had no morals and bad character.
Can you come by for lunch…
I'm hoping you can analyze my data
and relieve my stress.
The analytical chart shows
that a little help is needed, and it's
not all that bad, but I want the best.
Maybe you can bend the curve in the right direction.
I call you because you are my true asset…when I'm surrounded by all these
liabilities.
I believe in scarcity…
But when I see you, you're all I want and need.
We look at my company, and we think of inflation because of the increase
in price…with your level of skill, the way you grind, and the way you work
it…I won't let inflation exist when it comes to you.
I mean look at you!
I'm at an absolute advantage
When it comes to competitors.
Your bread and butter,
your loyalty, and association with my brand have placed me at a competive
advantage.

I could have been a corporate raider or a brain drainer,
but Imma bootstrapping, with a callipygian at my side.
You know I used to tell people from my
country hometown of Greenville, Alabama,
that I would go all the way.
Too bad they didn't believe me.
I used to lose sleep and stress
because of my conflict of interest.
People were always lying and cheating me,
but God helped me and you helped me, so I got my z-score up!
I'm so blessed to be able to have a meeting discussing my business from A to
Z, from analytics to my z-score.
We have come along way...if somebody was hearing this conversation or
"READING IT," they would need to look up the words...
With that said, let's toast to new life...

And You Wonder Why

you tricking off a lot of people
And you wonder why I treat you different
you say you love me, but my Facebook timeline show you kissing another
And you wonder why I treat you different
you told everybody I ain't shit
And you wonder why I treat you different
you have never respected or accepted any of my ideals or passions
And you wonder why I treat you different
you don't pick up when I call
And you wonder why I treat you different
many nights I search for your love only to be rejected
And you wonder why I treat you different
now that I have found somebody else
you wonder why…It's because they treat me different…

Free Wi-Fi

My phone bill ain't paid, it's Tuesday, I got a quarter tank of gas, and I don't get paid till Thursday...

I said my phone bill ain't paid, it's Tuesday, I got a quarter tank of gas, and I don't get paid till Thursday...

The only thing I seem to think about is you...but I have no way to touch base with you...the only method I know of is free Wi-Fi,

so I run out into the rain...hop in my car...and speed

relentlessly until I see a free Wi-Fi sign...the first thing I see is a McDonald's...with free Wi-Fi,

so I park and go inside...unfortunately, a lot of the people on this shift are a little ignorant...

but this employee named Monique

won't interfere with what I got goin' on.

As I sit here and converse on Facebook...I think about how great of a person you are

and how time flies when we talk.

I'm just here for the free Wi-Fi;

I don't want to be bothered.

No, I don't want a sloppy burger, a shake, or french fries; I just want to imagine her smile and beautiful brown eyes...Free Wi-Fi.

Dopeboy

People act as if drug dealing is as fun
as stocks and bonds.
But this is my life…and for survival,
we gotta take chances.
You watch tv and develop sterotypes of me.
You see, when I first started, my mother was sick, and I couldn't afford
medicine…so goddammit, I had to do something…
because even Obama Care couldn't help me on top of my two full-time jobs
with overtime.
Imagine being helpless,
being born in the depths of society.
I don't have credit nor the friends or assets to make her better.
Every day I cry, and my life full of adrenaline…because them jack boys
are plotting;
they trying to take my head off for the love of the green because, conse-
quently, they suffering from the same thing.
The weed is from the earth, so it has
more positive qualities than negative qualities.
By your standards, it's wrong, but by
mine, it's an Avenue to make things right, so catch me if you can.
I could do a lot time, but to get my daughter through college is enough for
me…just to know she ain't gotta go through what I been through…
All I see is where she's goin' to, and
I refuse for her to be a fool, so it's a chance for her to go to lawyer or doctor
school.

You drive by and frown on me
when, actually, you doin' the same thing selling cigarettes, which cause
cancer,
and beer that destroys the liver, kidney, and brain...that's actually worse.
As time has progressed, my daughter has graduated college,
and I have turned my illegitimate activity into positive businesses. You
spend your whole day worried about me...when we got murderers and rap-
ists out there...
I turned away from that life.
But do you define me as bad?
I was able to get my mother the medicines she needs, and she's cured.
Ironically, the hospital had prescribed her marijuana for her condition.
I ask do you dislike me?
Recently I started a nonprofit organization for others who suffered the
same, and I give away scholarships every year.
My house is paid off, and we live comfortable.
Question is, am I a respectable man?
Or just trash that just came up out the life I was given?
You can judge, but
at this point in life, I'm doing more for the world than you ever have...God
forgives me...will you?

My Resume

I heard you were looking for somebody to fill the position, so I put in my application.

Lately I've heard of people walking out on you and not completing or doing a good job.

This position is all I've ever wanted.

So if I'm eligible, I want to apply.

I been around the world, and I have hands-on experience.

The description says that you're looking for someone reliable, on time, and dedicated to giving you the maximum.

I'm always on time, and you won't be disappointed.

If you give me a chance, I won't ever let you down.

I guarantee to be better than any other employee who left you overwhelmed.

I'm looking to start today.

I want to be the man who puts a smile on your face when I enter into your presence and thoughts.

Hire Me, Please.

What Don't You See

I'm not conceited, but goddamn!
Are you blind?
You single, but you chasing a dude
with no job who don't care about nothing.
I'm so mad you don't see yourself.
You went to college for years and bust your butt just to date a guy with no
ambitions, who sits on the sofa, plays the video game all night, and lives
off your work.
I've come to grasp that you don't know what you want or what you need,
so you go out to open mics and poetry nights just to find something real
when it's right in front of you.
Or sometimes right beside you.
Instead of giving the right African American a chance, you say we all bad
and go find a Caucasian...
Ol' house nigga, why not find you
somebody Korean or Mexican? A brother could pay your bills, change your
tires, take you to work, repair feelings that were hurt, save you like Captain
Kirk, take you out for dinner and dessert, help you forget about that jerk,
let you treat him like dirt, actually show you he the best, compliment your
hair or dress, take your kids to school,
and you'll tell your friends he's a fool.
You gotta wall full of awards and college degrees, but can't notice a good
man bowing down on his knees, begging to do what you please...
Why can't you see what's right in front of you?

Black Bird

I sat outside one day, and I saw a black bird fly by.
As the bird flew by, it came back and landed.
I wanted it nowhere near me,
so I left the area...
I laughed then began to wonder what a black bird's day was like.
Unlike other birds, the black was never embraced through the years by society.
People often associated the black bird with death.
It has the ability to fly at high and low speeds...being a beautiful creature in our society, not many realize the inner beauty of this bird.
We typically fear it 'cause it's black.
The black bird arguably is under attack more than any other bird, even by birds.
Regardless of its dangers, it still boldly flies in the presence of few friends and many enemies to feed its children and ensure their survival until the black bird eventually dies.
But before it dies, it teaches its babies how it accepts itself and still flies high and beautiful,
regardless of the hatred many have toward it because black is not a color they like.
As I imagined the condition of the black bird...I realized we are in the same position.
I feel sorry for the poor little black bird...
So how should I feel about myself...
Oh, that's right...HIGHLY and BEAUTIFUL.

Can I be your Mechanic?— The Mechanic

My mind begins to wonder
as I imagine how it would be to thrust my key into your ignition,
to accelerate...until your body shakes and your engine roars...
To feel your vibrations makes me feel like a man.
To see the results of this tune-up
would let me know that I'm doing my job.
You'd tell your friends that I work that drag strip
like a professional, and that I know just how to switch your gears.
R. Kelly says you remind him of his jeep, but he don't know nothing.
Truth is...you remind me of my sports car.
I wanna drift, slide, lean, and speed into you.
And when it gets too dangerous, I want an emergency brake—I just wanna
take my hands off the nine and three o'clock position of the wheel
as you reverse, and I sit and watch.
I just need a test drive...because after my analysis, everything seems to be
great.
"Ma'am, are you OK?" Please give me your phone number and keys...

In the House

I want you to be young and free,
but I also want your ass to be in the house.
I'm not trying control you,
neither do I want to be controlled.
I just want a great understanding.
By being at the house, we gain more mobility in our relationship.
From time to time, it's cool for you
to kick it with Tasha, Tiffany, and Kim,
but Imma tell you straight up: I don't like the rest of them.
But as long as it doesn't interfere with us, I can accept them.
Babe, we are hardworking individuals
with dreams that we are approaching more every day.
Maybe I can get you that condo in Miami or LA.
But the things we do today
pave the way for tomorrow,
so let's love each other like there is no tomorrow.
I found out you were with another
man. . .I'll try my best to understand.
Maybe we can find out your reason why
you're not here with me.
People keep telling me
you're a gold digger and a hoe,
but that I don't believe!
I only see a queen, and if you hurry back home, we can plan to achieve.
I know you with your friends; tell the rest of them I said hi.

Until then, I'll be in the house,
and I'll probably be asleep
because I know you having a good
time.
Don't worry about the number and the jacket I found at the house; I'm sure
you can explain it.
Until then, I'm alone, 'cause my friends think I'm crazy...so I'm "In the
House."
I love you...hit me up...where are you?

I Ain't Your Toy

I ain't your toy that you have
for leisure when everything else goes wrong.
I ain't your toy that you have
when life beats you down and you're not feeling so strong.
I ain't your toy
that you find when all the real niggaz, bitches, and hoes are gone.
I ain't your toy that you can
just run over like a safety cone.
I ain't your toy that when things get rough you run to like a safety zone.
I ain't your toy that you find
like a hidden dog bone after your
evenings have been filled with the wrong Deandres, Quezes, and Tyrones.
I ain't your toy when you trying to escape the smell of cigarillos and cheap
five-dollar cologne.
I ain't your toy
when your man ain't at home—I'd flip out if I was him and you did me
the same way while I was gone.
I ain't your toy that you use
when you wanna moan; they sell that stuff in stores, online, and on the
phone.
I ain't your toy, but I want to be your
man, so stop addressing me as a boy,
or leave me the hell alone.
'CAUSE I'M GROWNNNN…I ain't no toy.

Black Power

It is true the sun
empowers our skin,
but real black Power starts from within?
I'd like to ask, what is black Power?
I'd like to ask again: what is black Power, my brothers, sisters, and friends?
Is it taking pride in selling or using drugs,
or is it loving everyone
with kisses or hugs?
Is it degrading our women with words of hurt like bitch, whore, or thot?
Is it putting the next brother down
because you want his spot?
I ask, where is the power in social media with sisters half naked, and brothers throwing money just to see them shake it?
Why does almost every piece of black art have a half-naked man or woman on it? Do we not believe in clothes? Is black Power consistently, day in and day out, making excuses for your failures or shortcomings?
Is black Power being the only nigga on a job surrounded by white folks?
Is black Power not respecting yourself morally in society regardless of the risk that comes with it?
Is black Power being a father who doesn't respect his baby mother or provide for his children?
Is black Power being a mother who hates the child's father, and when he calls, you don't bother to answer the phone 'cause YOU hate the father?
Is black Power a crutch that people use 'cause they too scared to stand up in a failing society?

29

Some people scream black Power and don't know the true meaning.
A lot of those people use black Power as a way to seek revenge.
Some people use black Power as a way to cause destruction, demise, and could bring all us to an end.
Some people use black Power for all the right reasons.
Some people use black Power to make money on products like food seasonin'.
Some people use black Power as a way to convince or reason.
If we have black Power,
let's put our kids through college, let's have seminars and share knowledge.
Let's inspire the next generation; let's stop all these innocent killings.
If you believe in black Power, then let's start on shaping our children,
because black Power is being the best black you could possibly be and inspiring others around you to do the same.
Don't get it twisted; it's a way of life,
not just a saying, not a playing, or an MF game. BLACK POWER.

Hot Pursuit—The Getaway

Calling all units:
Be advised there is a good
woman on the loose.
She has put up with so much in life that she is running away from what
she deserves.
She is as innocent as a newborn.
She assumes I want to continue to hurt her like she was in the past.
Out of fear, she has sped away, scared of the circumstances that might come
into effect.
I merely want to stop her and tell her I understand where she is coming from
or what she is going through.
Before I could express my words,
she took off.
She came from an abusive relationship
and feels like things won't get better.
She has tried constantly to do right, but everything and everybody continue
to fail her—I see a potential leader and a great woman who has endured
quite a bit of hurt,
and I swear to God, if any of you hurt her, you will get what you deserve.
I'm gaining on her.
I guess she sees me in her rearview, 'cause she's trying to fake me out . . .
but I've been here in life; I know exactly where she going.
Everybody stand down; I got her under control.
I REPEAT: all units stand down.
She has come to a stop.

She has thrown all her baggage out the window, and she has stopped crying. I think she's coming back to reality and what is best for her.

I have yelled to her to meet me halfway...be advised we both are running toward each other...so stand by.

We are hugging, and I can hear her heart "BOOM." Wait! Why did you shoot her in the back? She had no weapon...I had it under control...Oh my God, you just killed a good woman...All units, be advised: a good woman died today...proceed to your regular duty...as I mourn losing her.

F' Me

Today I don't have time for a love potion or to love like Trey in slow motion.
I'm not thinking 'bout
the stars or the ocean,
no Bath & Body Works
or lotions.
I want you to FUCK ME
like you want a promotion.
I want to cause a big commotion
anywhere we go make motion.
I wanna make you sweat
while I choke you from
the back of your neck
and pound your backside
until we flip, and you ride
until you tired.
Girl you better fuck me, or you might get fired. Do your job right, or you
gonna see a Signs saying "Now Hiring".
I'm just kidding.
You're so fine it's inspiring. I love sex, so when I stroke, I know I can last
for a while.
Like Mickey Ds, I love to see you smile.
Don't hold back; you know I like it rough.
Don't tease me; take your clothes off.
Strip down and let me go down
while you make oooo ahhh sounds.

No dress or skirts, just skin.
We are more than just lovers and friends.
When I beat you sexually,
one might think we boxing.
I wanna make you sweat.
I wanna make you wet.
I won't have to ask, have you came yet?
'Cause who can love you like me?
Not even Keith Sweat.

Hell Nawl

Dude came to me smelling like loud
asking for the hand of my daughter
who I see like Penny Proud.
There're millions of men out there—why he think he the one out the crowd?
Man, HELL NAWL!
Dude ask me to borrow some money till Sunday...that he get paid on Monday
...but I heard he was at the club doing donuts in a new Hyundai...
Man, HELL NAWL!
She don't cook no food, wash no dishes, make no love, clean no part of the house, or pay no bills, but she asking for some Michael Kors.
Girl...HELL NAWL...put that shit down.
He ask me, have you been drinking? I said HELL NAWL.
He ask me, did you know you were speeding...I said HELL NAWL.
Point is, folks keep asking me all these damn questions, but they know good and well Imma say HELL NAWL...

I Don't Know If I'm Ready

She says Baby don't call my phone
just to play with my emotions,
but, ironically, others have done the same thing to me.
They say every action has a repercussion, so why the fuck am I crying or
even having this discussion?
I'm thinking bout calling her and saying, fuck it, let's be together.
The fact that I'm writing this poem lets me know that we could be together.
I call her every day just to tell her my problems, but I'm scared to ask for
more because things never turn out right...
Who am I...when I stare into the mirror,
romantically I see another nigga
who's scared to love,
hurt by past hoes lusting for money, cars, and clothes.
I'm writing a poem...with tears in my
eyes 'cause I criticize other guys, but now another stares into your eyes.
While you make love, he grips your thighs.
It's like every brother wanna be balling like they in the NBA...living the
wrong way, not caring for the next day.
Seems like we mistake affection for gay
when it's time to be strong men who lead the way.
Our generation is a disappointment to Lenny Williams, Al Green, and
Marvin Gaye.
Here I have a woman who loves me unconditionally and in an infinite way,

but I couldn't find it in my heart to love back.
Now o boy loving that.
And I can't do a damn thing about it except accept that,
because I wasn't ready.

Cocaine—Confessions of a Sex Junkie

I'm handsome, so women undress me with they eyes.
They say, come here boy and get in-between these thighs.
When I get into they domain
and start doing my thing,
I find myself on an emotional high.
The sex is like cocaine.
Well, the strawberries is like cocaine—
strawberry cocaine.
Sex ain't never hurt me,
but it's unhealthy to fill desires of women who don't deserve me.
They truly unworthy,
but sex so good,
we fiend for a hit like cocaine,
and when we get it, we come to
explosions like propane.
I make her body sang;
when she rides this mustang,
she moans and screams
and says, boy you know you doin' ya thang.
As long as I keep getting they cocaine,
I have no reasons to complain.
In the shadows, I'm everything.
My neighbors are impressed

and even know my name.
What's the need for a wife or a wedding ring
when I can make
all bridesmaids sing?
Why? Y'all trippin', the groomsman doing the same thing.
I want success, a wife, and a child,
but for now, I got cocaine, and it's everything.
I'm forever free, flapping my wings,
and hopefully I won't die chasing that cocaine...when life is filled with a
lot better things...can I get some of your cocaine.

I Never Would've Thought

I never would've thought that we were once kings and queens.

I never would've thought that we were once slaves to whites and other races...because most of the hurt and self-conflict is among the black faces. Y'all need to get ya mind right.

I never would've thought I'd be writing a "we shall overcome" speech; well, I'm not, 'cause we gonna overcome.

I never would've thought when I was a kid that we would grow up to all these black-on-black crimes with

glorified trap lives of nickels and dimes.

I never would've thought that every time y'all wanted to be the best you can be, you bring up MLK. Truthfully, he had a dream...that we are yet to live.

With all the innocent that are killed,

it's amazing the guilty still live.

I never would've thought

I would be such a significant leader among the people.

I never would've thought that my words hold so much meaning.

I never would've thought that I would have to help get an entire generation in order.

I never would've thought that our women would be called bitches.

I never would've thought that

It would be difficult to take my niece to get ice cream with so much disrespectful content on the radio.

I never would've thought I'd need a protecting weapon the way that I do.

However, somewhere in life, somebody never would have thought he'd die
for our sins.
They never would've thought Barrack Obama would become president
of the United States.
They never thought we would make a difference.

For One Night

I listened to Luther tonight, and I began to wonder if I just had one night, all the sexual or erotic thoughts, words, and actions I would take and say unto you.

I've just wanted to love you; for years, I've longed to be that man to embrace you in my arms at night,

to be in your thoughts from night to morning light.

I know you a married woman, but I just want to touch and love you all night.

This is a sin, but it feels so good,

even though it hurts to write

and think about 'cause it ain't right, but

when I see you, I see an Angel

who has lost its sight and its wings,

substituted by a rich man with material things and a nice-size wedding ring.

For you, I'd play my piano and sing

songs about sex, love, and pain—'cause I want you as my woman,

not as a boo thang.

Asking you to run away from home is a difficult thing to try to explain,

but he doesn't love you like I do,

and he doesn't spend the time—his words are abusive, and anything but kind.

I know you not a cheater, but you deserve more than McDonald's, take out, and fajitas,

people sucking out your life
like mosquitos.
I want just one night of music by Mrs. Anita while we laugh and sip
margaritas,
and if the night is still young,
then we could watch TV and eat Dorito's, and if you really wanna turn up,
then we can break out Stevie Wonder and tequila.
I see your worries and fears,
and it hurts me to know that one night
won't wipe away your hurt and tears. I ask for one night...but for your
hand I'd fight 'cause you living wrong, and I just wanna make things right.
And if it feels all right,
we can start with tonight...

If All Women Were Like Oprah

A life full of misfortune,
raped at nine with dreams still on mind,
pregnant at fourteen,
probably thinking, "What will everybody think of me?"
But they don't know it was forced upon me by friends and people kin to me.
What makes it even worse,
she lost a child in infancy,
was having to deal with the issues
deep down in Mississippi but was raised in Milwaukee. The legendary
Oprah Winfrey is everything to me:
the Queen of All Media and
her name travels around the world like Expedia.
She tried drugs to escape certain things that weighed heavy on her heart
and brain; after all, she even lost a sister to cocaine.
Simple words can't explain the strength of this African American woman.
She approaches life the same as Serena when she enters the arena.
The film Color Purple *inspires Wayne Brady, Ushers, to Steve Urkels:*
a film about pain and misery
has awakened people like a pizza man at your front door delivering.
She battled insecurities with weight and the word fat, but she lost that,
wore cheap clothes that looked like potato sacks
while others would point as if she was the only one to laugh at, but she
overcame and conquered all that.
She's the first female black billionaire
and could literally command life from a well-deserved beach chair,

because she's the richest self-made woman in America—oh yeah, the great-
est American and hands-down the most powerful and influential woman in
the world. And it all started with dreams from a lil girl.
I've determined life could be so much better
if women were more like Oprah Winfrey—never accepting failure.

Diamond

You would be amazed by the life I've lived; I've been used and abused.
When fighting for myself, people
often are confused...as if I shouldn't.
When I was on the road to success,
I ran out of gas...yet we was close.
My closest friends exited the vehicle and said, kiss my ass!
At this point I learned who was down
and who would never come or who not to have around.
So I've kept it one hundred and have realized
I gotta hold myself down.
And that day that I shine will come,
where my words will touch people as a way to mental and social freedom.
I'm angered to heats of Sydney
'cause those who talk bad about me look to me for a kidney in times
of need. I just think, "Are you kidding?"
I BEEN! living in misery. Although
I'm real, but there's no chivalry—when the rent money was due,
and I didn't have it...who could I depend on to come through..."not you!"
You see, in life, you gotta get cut to precision to be great, which is similar
to diamonds.
With decisions often come permanent circumstances or magnified ways to
advancement.
I have been cheated on, lied to, stolen from, and misunderstood.
With all that I have faced, I begin to wonder, how does a man stand tall?
Above all, I found that where most failed, I continue to keep faith,

traveling roads in life that ain't safe
because I want to be GREAT!
I cut on the TV and see some of my favorite entertainers with nice jewelry,
but I got something most of them don't—I have an internal glow.
You see, when the lights get low
or times get hard, a lot of people from our generation look to me to lead
because they know pressure can bust pipes or pressure can make diamonds,
and even under all the pressure they can still see me shining
JUST LIKE DIAMONDS.

How Can I Not Shine

I'm a star: how can I not shine?
God put me here to do great things,
but I dim my own lights to blend in with those who are suffering.
The situations they are currently facing, I have an in-depth education.
From trial and error I have learned my lessons, but if I speak up it might sound like Usher's "Confessions,"
but that's a good thing;
still, I'd rather not say nothing! 'Cause
I don't want to be judged! The pastor say Imma leader...I dunno, I kinda agree,
'cause when we in public, I feel that desire burning like a Holy Ghost fire when it touch the soul of a Sunday school church choir.
If I could just believe in myself, I could grand slam like Mark McGwire, or I could blow out like a bald tire.
If I stand, many won't like me.
You see, I only want to be loved—'cause I know I'm brilliant.
I could start by addressing how we all are political refugees to some extent, that the lies they tell are constant.
To fuel evil empires, there are liars
with forbidden desires.
I know they preaching about hope,
but we know they don't care about black folk.
You're all blinded by the screens of smoke falling for the okeydoke.
What's important, you can't see, 'cause
You're mentally blind in a world

that will provide you with mental vision, as long as you get out your feel-
ings and intuition.
If you wanna be a diamond, you gotta get cut like a circumcision.
Yeah, it might hurt for minute, but you'll be in a better position.
To open mouths like a dentist
To kill speeches like a menace
To bring fear like a gremlin
To be iconic in resemblance—to be a knowledgeable man
when the rest is chillen.
We all wanna ball, but who wanna fight?
Like Dragon Ball Z *Krillin,*
I ask, who will stand when others won't?
Who will stand when all are afraid?
Who will be the brave? Who gonna be the new slaves
when the world needs a star to lead the way toward a better day?

Mr. Glass

I'm down on my faith,
and I don't know why,
because you have protected me.
I remember being out chasing skirts, living a life full of dirt,
disregarding everybody's feelings,
not caring who gets hurt.
I smiled, but under my innocence
was a growing jerk.
I know I'm a great guy,
but I don't feel good when others' hearts get broke or feelings are hurt.
I think to myself, in several
situations, I could have died,
but you have protected me.
One time, one of my cars burst into flames under the hood,
but you led me and my best friend at the time to safety.
My mom suggested that I slow down,
but when times were rough,
you always held me down regardless who was around.
I constantly think about the night the front of my car got run over by a
truck.
I survived on a miracle,
but most call it luck.
People laughed as if I didn't go through that situation, suggesting I at-
tempted to almost kill myself for insurance money of about three stacks—
that I'd risk not coming back

for only THREE STACKS,
that I'd give my momma an asthma attack.
It's funny how when you hurting, the world still won't show you no slack.
That night in Montgomery, Alabama, I saw a tire fly over my windshield
and then an airbag that didn't deploy in my face.
I should have dropped to my knees and thanked you for sparing my life
then, because this was the type of situation that people become paralyzed,
set back, or either make movies or music videos about, but I stepped out my
car unhurt,
only to find out a couple of days later I suffered a concussion and minor
back injury. I couldn't believe that a woman victim to drugs came to my
crushed vehicle in flames and asked for five dollars mane. Later I found
that my wallet was missing. I can't prove she took it, but I was feeling very
unsure.
She might have been an Angel who distracted me from what really could've
happened.
I know my granny sent tears from heaven when she seen my car get balled
up. I can't complain about my ride or my backside. I had it easy—look
what happened to Yeezy.
Sometimes I wonder why I'm still breathing. I'm not too sensitive, but I
admit something like this gets to me.
It's powerful like an orchestra or a symphony. It's logical that I'm blessed or
heaven sent. I encourage others to say your prayers and repent.

Malcolm X—The Role Model

I want to be like Malcolm X,
protecting my people by any means
necessary; if the enemy bring that drama, Imma send them to the cemetery.
Ain't no time for no singing;
I'm simply swinging. If you bring aggression outside of a diplomatic
conversation,
I want to organize brothers in suits
like the Islam nation.
I want to empower black people
to teach them the
strengths of black Wall Streets,
to make OG's to geeks
understand we can be in power or command, if we stand tall and make
demands.
Vital are wars on the sand in Afghan,
but so is the war in America, since I'm African.
Too many black avoid the facts—passive lifestyles 'bout pussy, money,
weed,
but my philosophy is:
get it when you need it;
don't spend your whole life being excessive or exceeding.
Malcolm X would have a lot of speeches today,
'cause we ain't living the right way.
I'm ready for war, so I'm at my window with an AK.
I'm ready for a better day

where I can voice my opinion or show my intellect without hate or disrespect.
Malcolm X died young, but I'm sure it wasn't with regret or neglect...but
with respect:
a king who ruled on Earth,
a man who was prepared to walk on any turf on this earth,
and give birth
to independence.

Don't Cry When It Gets Hard

You outnumbered.
I said, you outnumbered!
It's only one of you.
You fighting with a desire,
researching like a chemist,
grinding like an apprentice,
because where you from
ain't no role models or symbols
except them dope niggaz,
and you can't define success,
but you know to stack some figures
so you can be like or
better than them niggaz.
You working overtime repairing credit,
but when they run it, they say, sorry, sir you just can't get it.
It's moments like this that empower your hustle, so don't forget it.
Invest in yourself, and you can get it,
even if you gotta use the debit. I know your circumstances,
but don't cry when it gets hard, my brother.
Take care of your lil sisters, brothers, and mothers.
Where you from, the infrastructure weak, a lot of real negus extinct
being passive and submissive at the wrong times.
They scared to be strong, firm, or even speak they mind.
So you gotta come through with that Nas 01 "Ether" spirit and mentality,
'cause in reality too many brothers

are in mortality,

only opinionated on the type of drinks, type of weed, and depending on
women to give them what they need.

If a man don't work, he don't eat,

but women love and believe,

so he gets the feed and a chance to beat her sweets, until one day
her stomach shaped unique.

From a beast, an innocent child is born oblique.

My brother, move with aggression.

Use your mind as a weapon.

Pave the path of truth.

Avoid deception or misconception.

But, my brother, don't cry when it gets hard,

even if you got to cut off the lights,

even if you gotta stand in the shower,

even if you gotta stand in the rain.

Don't let them see your pain

and never complain or be ashamed,

just conquer and do great things.

She Wasn't Ready

They were passing letters in high school.
The connection was simple and sweet:
she liked him, and he liked her.
He often thought what it would be like to hold her hand and walk in the
hallway while others stared at how great they looked together.
She felt like they could
be together forever.
As time progressed and they got to know each other, she saw that he was a
special, unique, and genuine brother,
and he saw the same in her. They were young and innocent, having good
intentions, but they didn't know how to love. As teens, they thought sex was
the only way to intervene.
One day he hit her up in her Facebook inbox; he asked for sex because his
family and friends laughed and peer pressured him into this, and he wasn't
ready. Most of them were saying he was too old to be a virgin when
half of them were.
She was scared and was a virgin also.
But her homegirl was like, it's easy, and continued to peer pressure her
about sex: she was like, I ain't gonna flex.
Just slide on a latex and wait for an orgasm next.
When he inboxed her, he said, I got my uncle's Chevy Friday night; let's hook up.
She said, we could go to my house, but my mama gonna be home. He said,
mine gon be home, too, so let's have sex in the Chevy. They loved each other
and were on each other's hearts heavy.
So she snuck out the house late,

*said she was goin' to her friend's house, but her friend was in a Challenger
at the party with an older man
and continued to say, it's easy and feel good, especially if he gonna buy you
stuff or if he got bands.
They arrived at the party after she snuck out the house.
Once they got to the parking lot, he started to kiss her in all the right spots
until she got hot. Then he tried to find a nice song on the radio, 'cause even
though she was hot, she still wasn't ready, he thought.
He was trying to set the mood right.
Once he got it right, he struggled to put on a condom. He tried to push it on. . .
then she tried to push it on, but they googled it, and it said, roll it on. . .
Once it was on, he entered her and thought to himself. . .is this really all sex
is about? Surely it feels good and she's beautiful, but is this what has all my
family and friends captive, ruining lives, careers, and futures?
He looked at her as she enjoyed him, but at the same time in tears and fear
about how she would be viewed if people found out she lost her virginity
in a car. He immediately stopped in the middle of sex and said, I want to
wait.
Then a song by Janet Jackson called "Let's Wait Awhile" came on the radio.
The lyrics were, "Let's wait awhile before we go too far."
They then cuddled in a blanket in the back seat of his uncle's Chevy and
began to talk about their future and mapped out their life goals, insisting
sex would come later. They then looked in the Challenger next to them and
saw her friend giving oral sex and using drugs. . .they tried to talk to her
about living life and taking her time, but she didn't listen. . .today she has
drug problems, in a relationship, with a man who doesn't care, and a lot
of kids; but unlike her, they have a very successful business pertaining to
self-respect and safe sex. . .because they decided to respect themselves and
wait awhile.*

Red, White, & Blue

He said you fighting for the red, white, and blue, and they haven't done a
damn thing for you.
You think you are brave, but you a slave,
fighting toward a darker day,
that you a nigga and they don't care what you have to say,
that my actions are not of any form of
justice, that they only contribute to prejudice.
Then I halted the conversation
with the words I GET IT!
We have been enslaved, we have been naive and deceived,
but how dare you criticize me for wanting to be all I can be and for protecting my community?
We can rage war or strive for unity,
but unfortunately, I GET IT.
I'd like to ask, have you done your best?
Since what I do feeds your anger...go ahead, nigga, get it off your chest!
Last time I checked, the commander in chief is a resemblance of me,
but you're an athlete who criticizes me for being in the army
when your enemy puts you on TV,
tells you to run a ball for their amusement in hopes of being an MVP,
but Bitch! We the real MVPs.
If we didn't exist, history would repeat,
regardless if the flag was RBG or RWB,
but I GET IT!

You screaming to me, let's get back to trapping, but tell me how that's proactive.

I'm no dermatologist, but that won't help my skin or what's within.

Just like together the colors of a rainbow make the world a more beautiful place, the actions of all people contribute to the vanity of their race.

Do YOU GET IT?

Regardless if you're here or there, your actions determine where you are Everywhere,

So let a real one get some air.

I Will Always Love You

When we first started, we were young and naïve,
playing T.I you can have whatever you like.
I had aspirations but wasn't quite living that life.
But I felt if I could get you,
I could change my circumstances
of being single and lonely to having a wife.
A kid so in a rush to fall in love, even
if it meant being phony.
I had promises of holy matrimonies,
but times were so rough, sometimes I couldn't afford baloney.
From this relationship built on lust, we
denied a lot of principles, including trust.
Going out on dates or anywhere was difficult for us, in front of friends we
would argue or yell.
Everybody in our business 'cause they would tell.
What happened to us? Two love birds feeling like jailbirds.
The fights got worse, feelings got hurt.
I said you ain't shit; you treated me like dirt.
Signs and symptoms said it wasn't going to work.
I was doing bad on the job
'cause I worried about us at work.
From the relationship I got a lot of repossessions.
I got scars, cuts, and bruises:
some were physical, some were mental, and some were emotional.
I remained loyal and devoted,

and everybody knowed it.
Streets said you had my mind gone, but
I was convinced I was army strong.
I just wanted us to work and for everybody else to leave us alone.
Sometimes I cry at night to the same songs, reminiscing on the day you
up and gone. So bad I wanted to say how much I hate you, but truth is, I'll
always love you because you made me better.

No Longer

I broke up with a bitch
to get with an amazing chick
who devoted her life to me.
She would dance, sing, love, and cook for me.
It got to a point where we needed each other like a kidney.
Then one day, she thought she could say any type of shit to me.
She is no longer with me,
'cause the good ones go.

The Janitor

To you, I'm just a janitor.
Although my job title doesn't say that,
that's exactly how you feel,
because I use my hands to perform hard work and labor that most think too
highly of themselves to do.
My religion teaches me to be humble.
My religion teaches me
not to be so prideful,
and most certainly to lend a hand,
and provide that love
that God would provide.
The thing about life is most people result to classism once they exceed a
certain level in life.
I have no need to impress anybody.
You see, I work hard because God sees and judges my actions,
which, in reaction,
I get my blessings.
Some of you come by my job, and when I ask can I help, you look at me
like a deer in headlights.
Truth is, I want nice things for my family and me, and I don't mind putting
in a little work.
So while you laugh and make funny faces,
I'm stacking big faces.
I hustle hard while you complacent.
So when you see the house and the car I drive, you'll realize all the time
you wasting while you stuck up with you funny faces...

Send Me

Send me pics if you good looking.
Send me food if it's finger licking.
Make love to me if you need a good sticking.
Send my book in hashtags if it was an inspiration,
made you glad, or even mad.
Post pictures on your IG if you feel
you have built a connection with me.
Add me on Facebook and snapchat;
I promise to get back.
Salute me in the hood, 'cause a real nega
wrote a book, and it's doing good.
Send me booty pics and boob shots 'cause…
well, just 'cause.
Send me thank-you letters.
Send me hate-you letters. Whatever you send, make sure
it's well put together.
It's my first book; some say it's a masterpiece.
I say I can do better.
So do some of you.
So, in other words, be on the lookout for:

PROFESSIONAL LOVE PART II,
COMING SOON TO YOU.

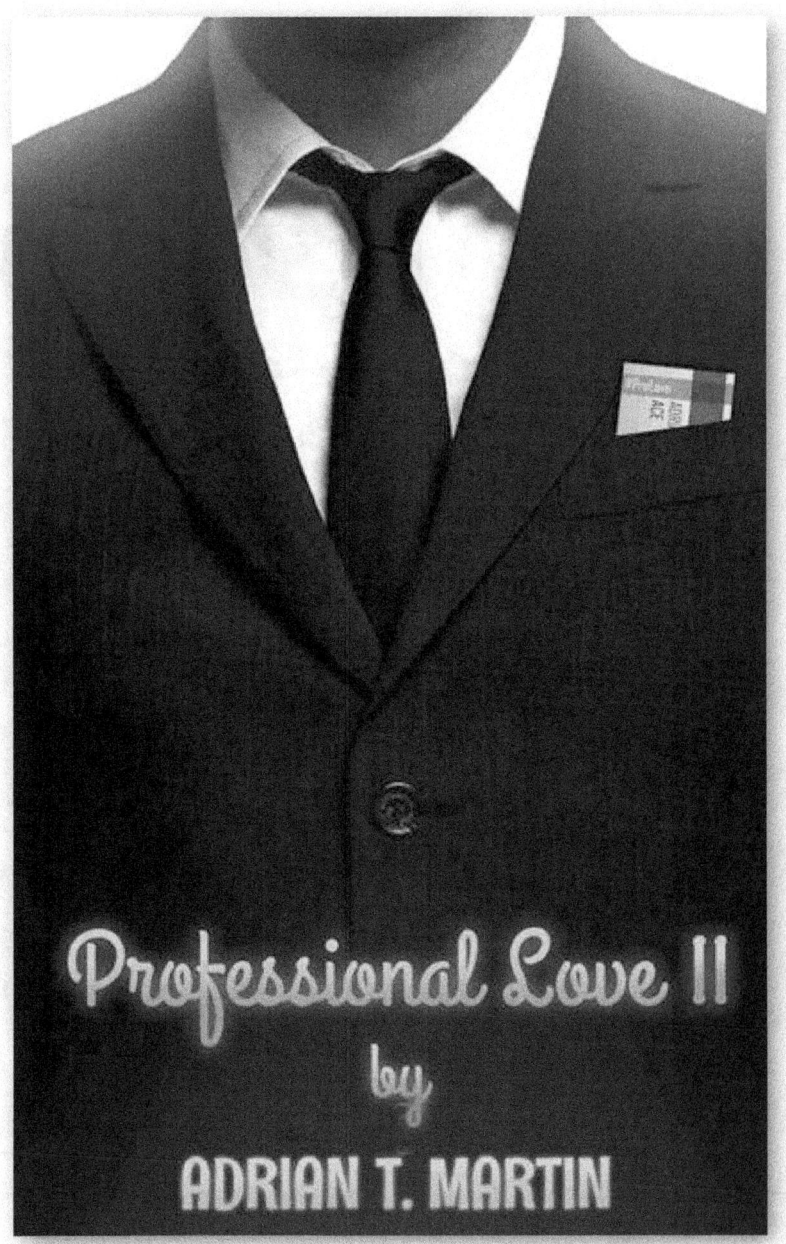

Professional Love II

by

ADRIAN T. MARTIN

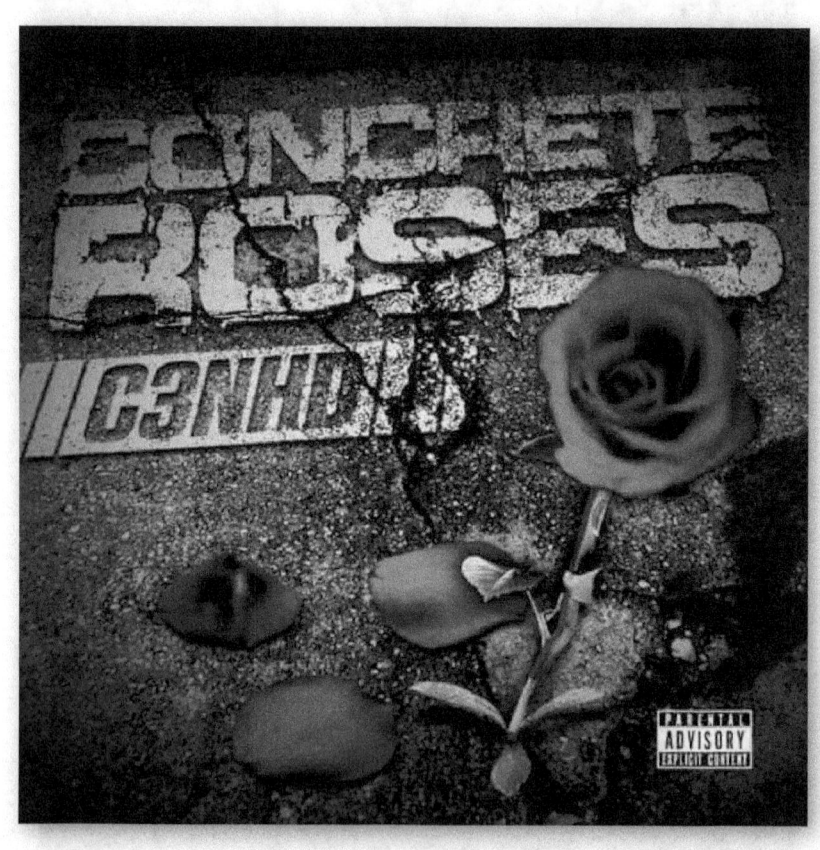

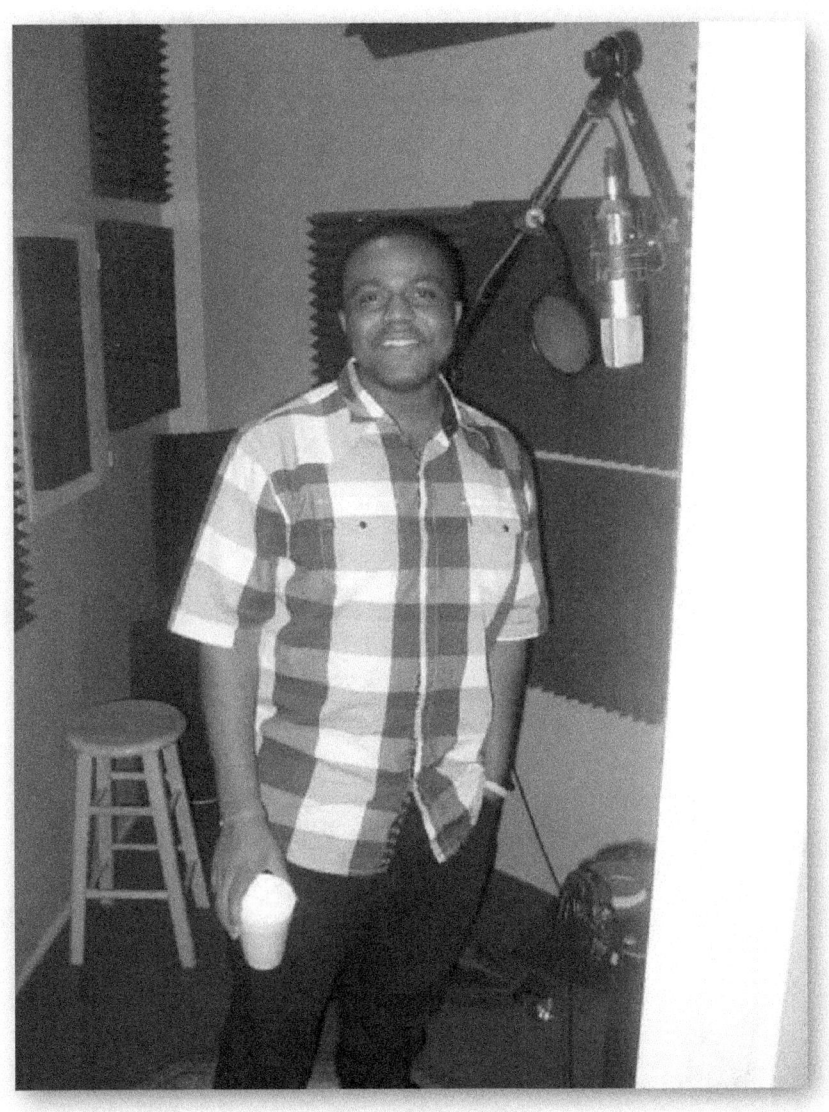

Forever In Our Hearts

Chris Terrell

www.ingramcontent.com/pod-product-compliance
Lightning Source LLC
Chambersburg PA
CBHW060411190526
45169CB00002B/854